The Little People's Guide To The Big World

WRITTEN AND ILLUSTRATED BY

TREVOR ROMAIN

The Little People's Guide to The Big World is dedicated to the children of Texas,
whose health and well-being are the primary focus of the
Texas Medical Association Alliance - Physicians' Spouses Joining to Care.

This book has been produced for the Texas Medical Association Alliance
as part of its Healthier Youth initiative.

Proceeds will be used to fund community service projects
on subjects such as substance abuse, teen pregnancy, child abuse, AIDS education, and others.

The Alliance would like to thank the review panel:
Beverlee Herd, Sandy Lanier, Robert Rogers, MD, Cathy Toledo, and Susan Rudd Wynn, MD,
for their direction; and
Travis County Medical Alliance for early assistance in the project's success.

Published By:
BRIGHT BOOKS
2313 Lake Austin Boulevard, Austin TX 78703 (512) 499-4164

Copyright © 1993 by Trevor C. Romain

ISBN 1-880092-04-2

For
Dumi
And
Miles

Way Cool is spokesman for the Texas Medical Association Alliance's Healthier Youth 2000 initiative.

TABLE OF CONTENTS

BULLY TROUBLE

Bullies are mean
bullies don't care
they pull on your ears
then pull on your hair

Bullies have problems
that make them real bad
sometimes they're lonely
or angry or sad.

Bullies enjoy
making you squirm
they want you to crawl
like a scared little worm.

Some bullies have gangs
that make them feel strong
If they head your way
you should move right
along.

Then tell your parents
or a trusted grown up
and they'll make sure
the bully will stop.

Don't feel ashamed
about turning them in
It's the only way
you can ever win

6

BEING NERVOUS

If you feel nervous
breathe through your nose
breathe deeply and slowly
then touch your toes.

Breathing this way
will soon help you out
it slows down your body
so you don't have to shout.

We all feel nervous
one time or another
and it helps to talk
to your father or mother.

HELPING OUT

We all do chores
it's part of life
for son and daughter
husband and wife.

Cleaning up
is always a pain
you have to do it
and do it again.

To make helping easy
call it a game
make up some rules
and give it a name.

Dirt and bugs
are bad for you
keep your room clean
that's what you should do.

Help your folks
try to be neat
when on clean floors
do have clean feet.

Do your chores
and do them well
and just by chance
your allowance might swell.

DANGEROUS THINGS

Guns and swords
and matches and knives
are dangerous things
that can end our lives.

Don't jump off the roof
don't play with fire
and whatever you do
don't touch a live wire.

If someone is playing
a dangerous game
just ignore them
and don't do the same.

Rather be careful
rather be scared
just walk away
if you are dared.

Then tell your parents
what happened to you
they'll check it out
and know what to do.

GETTING LOST

Getting lost
is not much fun
where should you go
where should you run?

The best thing to do
is stay where you are
your parents will find you
if you don't go too far.

If you're in a store
or a big shopping mall
ask a cashier
to give them a call.

A uniformed guard
can help you out too
he's well trained
and knows what to do.

Don't be too scared
don't get a fright
you'll feel a lot better
with your parents in sight.

When next you go out
decide where to wait
in case you get lost
or someone is late.

GOING TO THE HOSPITAL

Rest in the hospital
is not much fun
it's better to read
or play in the sun.

But hospitals help
the sick to get well
the nurses are nice
and the doctors are swell.

If you have to go
don't feel sad
it's not that scary
and not that bad.

Once you get better
and are all cured
you'll leave there quick
yes, rest assured.

LONELINESS

If you feel lonely
and empty inside
you just want to cry
or run out and hide,

speak to your mom
or speak to your dad
and they'll find out
what's making you sad.

Speak to your uncle
or speak to your teacher
if you really feel bad
you can speak to a preacher.

But if no one's around
to help you out
do a puzzle
or even shout.

Think of things
that make you smile
read a book
or draw for awhile.

Being by yourself
is sometimes fun
you can do it indoors
or in the sun.

Being alone
is not so bad
if you keep yourself busy
and happy and glad.

MOVING

Moving is fun
moving is sad
it can make you feel good
it can make you feel bad.

It's tough to leave
your friends behind
and you're never quite sure
what you're going to find.

What's great about moving
is seeing new places
meeting new friends
and exploring new spaces.

It's so hard to be
the new kid on the block
but it doesn't take long
to get over the shock.

You can write old friends
and phone them too
discuss what's happening
tell them what's new.

Before you know it
you'll be safe and sound
enjoying the bunch
of new friends around.

STRANGERS

Strangers are people
whom you don't know
if they come too close
just get up and go.

Don't talk to strangers
and don't take a ride
if they try to touch you
run fast and hide.

Find someone you know
or run to a store
if your parents aren't home
try the neighbor next door.

Don't walk alone
when you're out and about
and if someone approaches you
give a loud shout.

Sometimes strangers
look fine and okay
whatever they offer
you just say, "No way."

Need a ride?

Tell someone you trust
and tell them fast
remember the place
the stranger was last.

Ask mom and dad
the best thing to do
if a stranger should suddenly
come up to you.

AIDS

AIDS is a disease
that many will get
it cannot be cured
at least not yet.

It's not like a cold
or a cough or the flu
it's a deadly disease
that's bad through and through.

Some people have died
and many more will
until doctors can find
a shot or a pill.

If you meet someone with AIDS
don't worry too much
you cannot get AIDS
from people you touch.

Kids getting AIDS
is pretty rare
if they are cautious
and take some care.

Keep away from drugs
and let your parents tell
you how to be safe
and protect yourself well.

JEALOUSY

There's a certain feeling
that makes you feel bad
when someone has something
that *you* wish you had.

They call it being jealous
that feeling you get
it makes you irritable
it makes you fret.

Don't feel alone 'cause
it happens a lot
to all sorts of people
who want more than they've got.

But we can't always have
all that's in sight
if you enjoy what you've got
then you've seen the light.

CUTS AND SCRAPES

If you get cut or scraped
the first thing you should do
is to stop the cut from bleeding
and the germs from getting through.

Find yourself a tissue
and press where you are hurt
and when the bleeding stops
you should wash away the dirt.

It might sting a lot at first
but you need to get it clean
to wash away all of the germs
they are nasty and they are mean.

Then get yourself a band-aid
and cover up the cut
it will help protect the wound
and keep it tightly shut.

If it won't stop bleeding
there's one thing you must do
ask a friend or an adult
to get some help for you.

Once the scare is over
then the cut won't seem so bad
but make certain that you show it
right away to mom or dad.

STEALING

Stealing is easy
like telling white lies
but it's against the law
and not very wise.

Getting caught
can be very bad
it can hurt your life
and that's more than sad.

If you get caught
you might go to jail
where being indoors
will make you pale.

And when you get out
people will say,
"Here comes a thief,
let's get out of the way."

POLICE

Police are important
of that you can be sure
they help keep the law
and make us feel secure.

They arrest bad people
and stop cars for speeding
they call the ambulance
when people are bleeding.

Some people don't like them
and some people do
but without police
we'd be in a stew.

Imagine if gangs
were allowed to fight
and crazy criminals
walked free every night.

We wouldn't go out
we'd all be afraid
without the police
our freedom would fade.

Police are there
to help us out
if **you** are in need
just give them a shout.

In case of trouble
or emergency
Call 911
and report what you see.

Ask your mom or your dad
to tell you more
about 911
and what it is for.

19

DIVORCE

Sometimes parents
find it hard to be married
this makes them sad
and awfully worried.

They know deep down
they should be apart
and so they decide
to make a new start.

Divorce is the way
a marriage ends
parents who separate
often stay friends.

They still love their kids
divorced parents do
and no matter what happens
that love will be true.

They're still moms and dads
and exactly the same
they're just divorced
and no one's to blame.

SECRETS

When you hear a secret
don't tell a soul
keep it quiet
swallow it whole.

Tell it to no one
leave it inside
a secret's a secret
that you need to hide.

But sometimes a secret
can mean something bad
if it makes you feel funny
tell Mom or Dad.

The person who told you
will think it's not fair
but they might need some help
and it shows that you care.

Explain what you did
and tell why you told
I'm sure you'll stay friends
until you are old.

GLASSES

Wearing glasses
might make you sad
but if you wear them
don't feel too bad.

There are people with glasses
all over the place
just like your hair
they become part of your face.

It won't take too long
to forget they are there
and people won't see them
they won't even stare.

You'll feel a lot better
your eyes will too
you'll see more clearly
with a better view.

BURYING A PET

Sometimes a pet
will get old and die
it can make you lonely
you might even cry.

But that's part of nature
and all you can do
is remember the pleasure
the pet brought to you.

If your pet is a bird
or a fish or a mouse
you can bury the pet
behind your house.

Ask your parents
to give you a hand
then bury your pet
under some sand.

Mark the place
and say a small prayer
leaving a memory
that will always be there.

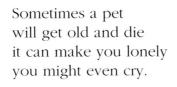

Here Lies Bubbles

TROUBLE

The trouble with trouble
is trouble itself
it's waiting to happen
it's bad for your health.

If you see trouble
heading your way
turn right around
and be sure not to stay.

Trouble needs friends
people like you
so that it can do
what it wants to do.

Try to ignore it
let it pass by
don't mess with trouble
don't even try.

RACISM

No matter where you live
no matter what you do
you'll see all kinds of people
who are different from you.

Many are of color
some don't speak the same
others have an accent
or a funny-sounding name.

You might have heard bad things
about those who aren't like you
that they are mean and dangerous
but that's not fair not true.

The world is full of people
good ones and bad
but to judge them by their color
is hurtful, dumb and sad.

If someone says mean things
about your religion or your color
it's best to walk away
and not to even bother.

These people have small minds
and not much else to do
except to say mean things
and write about them too.

But imagine just how boring
the world would really be
if people all looked much the same
there'd be nothing new to see.

We learn from other people
about many kinds of things
that can help us join together
to face what the future brings.

Remember one small thing
that hating hurts you too
it closes up your mind
to what's honest and what's true.

SAYING GOOD-BYE TO A FRIEND

Sometimes friends
have to move away
although you wish
so much they could stay.

There's nothing worse
than saying good-bye
it makes you sad
it makes you cry.

But listen up
there's something good
you'll have an *old* friend
in a *new* neighborhood.

You can visit
you can call
no need to worry
no need at all.

Because friends stay friends
through thick and thin
no matter what they do
no matter where they've been.

NIGHTMARES

Nightmares are dreams
that scare you at night
when it's dark outside
and you've turned off the light.

You wake up scared
with a wild beating heart
the nightmare disturbed you
and gave you a start.

Sometimes a hug
can make it all right
it helps you to sleep
right through the night.

Nightmares can come
from various places
like watching a movie
with frightening faces.

Also from worries
deep in your head
that only come out
when you're asleep in your bed.

When nightmares occur
the best thing to do
is tell you parents
what's bothering you.

27

MONEY

Money is great
money is funny
money can turn
a rainy day sunny.

If you need more
more than you've got
sell lemonade
when the weather is hot.

If the weather is cool
and sales are slow
when you need the cash
because funds are low,
try raking leaves
or cleaning a car
these little chores
will take you far.

Create your own job
like helping the old
walk someone's dog
so they won't be cold.

As long as you work
you'll definitely earn
and at the same time
you'll do a good turn.

Money is scarce
It can't grow on trees
but you earn it yourself
so can spend what you please.

Just put some away
in a little jar
so when you're sixteen
you can buy a car.

FAILING A TEST

If you fail a test
don't sit there and cry
you can always do better
the next time you try.

There are many people
some famous ones too
who looked at their tests
and hadn't a clue.

The world won't end
if you make a mistake
just prepare yourself more
for the tests that you take.

VISITING THE DOCTOR

(A very similar poem to Visiting The Hospital)

Going to the doctor
is not much fun
it's better to read
or play in the sun.

But the doctor helps
the sick to get well
they're always nice
and the nurses are swell.

If you have to go
don't feel sad
it's not that scary
and not that bad.

SELFISH

Just to show you how a person can be selfish...
I am not going to do a drawing
or even write a poem on this page.

TEASING

Teasing is nasty
and hurts people too
it's easy to do
'til it happens to you.

When the tables turn
and you are the one
you won't like being teased
while others have fun.

Soon you will see
that teasing is bad
it brings people down
and makes them feel sad.

If there's nothing good
that you want to say
just keep your mouth shut
and leave it that way.

HURT FEELINGS

Sometimes people
say things to you
that are mean and ugly
and often not true.

And what they say
makes you feel so bad
that you just want to cry
and get really mad.

The best thing to do
is pretend you don't care
that they hurt your feelings
and weren't fair.

Try to keep smiling
and don't show your pain
they'll soon get bored
and not hurt you again.

Often we say things
that hurt deep inside
and as soon as we say them
we wish we could hide.

So say what you mean
and mean what you say
and always think
before blabbering away.

MANNERS

Be polite
and respect the old,
listen to teachers
and do what you're told.

Don't interrupt
when people are speaking,
if something is private
there shouldn't be peeking.

Cover your mouth
when you're going to yawn,
obey all signs
like *keep off the lawn.*

Try not to talk
with a mouth full of food,
be well behaved
and don't be rude.

Don't burp, don't spit
and don't pick your nose,
be true to your friends
and don't step on their toes.

DRUGS

Drugs are awful
they play with your brain
they make you feel weird
they drive you insane.

If someone says
that drugs can't hurt
just think of the addicts
who live in the dirt.

Drugs steal your life
and mess with your soul
wearing you down
is their only goal.

Don't take a chance
just pass them by
even if good friends
beg you to try.

35

SMOKING

Some people smoke
don't ask me why
it's the grossest thing
you could ever try.

It hurts your body
and makes you stink
It's not as great
as you might think.

Smokers will tell you
it's cool to smoke
but if you ask me
it's all a big joke.

How can it be cool?
How can it be fun?
Tell them no way
if they offer you one.

Yes, **more** people die
from smoking the leaf
than anything else
that could bring us such grief.

36

DEALING WITH DEATH

When someone you love
suddenly dies
everyone hurts
and everyone cries.

It helps to talk
to your mom or dad
about the person
and the life they had.

Sometimes it's better
things happen that way
for those who are sick
and in pain every day.

It's not your fault
if someone is dead
don't let that thought
enter your head.

Death is sad
for grown-ups too
it doesn't seem fair
and hurts through and through.

It can make you angry
it can make you reel
but the more time passes
the better you'll feel.

When you think of that person
say a small prayer
and know that the memory
will always be there.

TALKING TO PEOPLE WHO CARE

If *you* feel bad
or unhappy inside
and need to discuss
the feelings you hide,

Talk to your family
or talk to a friend
don't keep it in
until the end.

Talking helps
to bring things out
things that frustrate you
and make you shout.

Talking is great
it opens your mind
it often solves problems
and helps you unwind.

There are people who care
who are waiting for you
to help you with problems
and make dreams come true.

BABY-SITTERS

If your baby-sitter
does something wrong
and acts kind of strange
while your parents are gone.

Like has weird friends
that come to your home
who drink and smoke
and sit on the phone.

Don't be afraid and
don't be upset
but it's very important
that you don't forget.

To tell mom or dad
make sure that they know
what the sitter does
after they go.

TOUCHING IN THE WRONG PLACE

If someone touches you
in a place that isn't right
tell them you don't like it
resist with all your might.

Don't be afraid to say it
even if they seem okay
just ask them not to touch you,
in any private way.

Be sure to tell your parents
tell them right away
because they know what's best
and they know what to say.

You are not to blame
if people touch you there
just make certain that you tell
exactly when and where.

The place that we call private
where people shouldn't touch
is right inside your bathing suit
and underwear and such.

GETTING SICK

Getting sick
is not much fun
but it happens sometimes
to everyone.

It's not that great
to stay in bed
with a drippy nose
or a pain in your head.

You can't go out
you feel really blah
you take some medicine
and say aaahhh..

But time passes by
and soon you feel right
no sneezing by day
no coughing by night.

Get plenty of rest
and stay indoors
keep out of damp places
and off of cold floors.

Keep yourself busy
with a book or a game
and before you know it
you'll be better again.

PUNISHMENT

If you are punished
for something bad
you'll probably feel angry
and get really mad.

It's pretty normal
to feel that way
whenever you're grounded
and don't get to play.

But give it some thought
and ask yourself why
you planned something bad
then gave it a try.

Punishment can happen
a reminder for you
to think very carefully
about all that you do.

"Blah, blah blah!"

"Blah, blah blah blah to you too!"

WHEN YOUR PARENTS FIGHT

Moms and dads
can argue too
they also get angry
like me and you.

If they fight
and scream and shout
just carry on playing
you can even go out.

They're letting off steam
and sorting things out
it sometimes helps
to scream and shout.

They still love each other
and also love you
they just argue sometimes
yes, that's what they do.

CHEATING

Cheating is wrong
it's like telling a lie
you don't want to do it
don't even try.

Don't cheat at school
nor in a game
all it will do
is dirty your name.

You'll feel like a fool
your face will turn red
and you'll look for a place
to hide your head.

FIRE

If you're at home
and a fire breaks out
let everyone know
by giving a shout.

Walk don't run
in case you might fall
and once you're out
give the firemen a call.

If the room fills with smoke
and you're still indoors
get close to the floor
and crawl on all fours.

The reason to crawl
is not a joke
it's just easier to breathe
under the smoke.

If your clothes are on fire
don't delay
roll on the floor
until the fire goes away.

Don't stop for a thing
not a pet, not a pan
just get out of the house
as quick as you can.

Don't fight the fire
it's stronger than you
just make sure that you're safe
that's the best thing to do.

45

GETTING BURNED

If you touch something hot
and feel yourself burn
take ice and cold water
and use them in turn.

Ice on the wound
will help it to heal
the quicker you do it
the better you'll feel.

Your mom or dad
can take it from there
if the burn feels bad
and needs further care.

46

And now I will rest
after writing this book
thanks for buying it
or just taking a look.